James Berney

Poems and Brief Sayings

James Berney

Poems and Brief Sayings

ISBN/EAN: 9783337888619

Printed in Europe, USA, Canada, Australia, Japan

Cover: Foto ©Andreas Hilbeck / pixelio.de

More available books at **www.hansebooks.com**

POEMS

AND

Brief Sayings

BY

JAMES BERNEY, Jr.

———— — ————

BEAR & LEASURE, Publishers,
BRADFORD, PA., 1894.

PREFACE.

THE AUTHOR of this little collection of poems and brevities regrets that it is not more extensive, but there are two sufficient reasons for restricting my book in size. The first is that the cost of publishing a book is very much greater than one would think, unless he had some little experience in such matters, and since my publishers, Messrs. Bear & Leasure, were so kind and liberal as to undertake its publication at their own risk, I thought best not to make the risk too great by the publication of a larger book, but let this little book suffice for an introduction to the public.

The other reason is that very much of my writing or work is very radical in its nature, and not calculated to please all, and so might offend some who have shown me kindness in my present affliction. I am only too glad to confess my deepest gratitude for the kindness which has been shown me by all classes of men and women.

I rejoice in the dawn of a better day wherein we all recognize, not the *Devilhood* of God, but that higher and better concept, the *Fatherhood* of God, and the motherhood and sisterhood of woman.

JAMES BERNEY, JR.

IN PERPLEXITY.

'TWAS on a very mild November eve,
    Chill winter lent a short but kind reprieve,
I wandered lone among the Tuna hills,
And sadly mused on life, its good and ills.
Among those hills that lately bloomed so fine,
I traced a life that much resembled mine.
For back to Spring 'twas but a little span
When in their midst, new life and joy began.
The tender buds were putting gently forth,
And joy prevailed o'er such a won'drous birth.
Here courting pheasants drum'd the live long day,
The cheery robin sang his roundelay;
The blackbird carrolled by yon winding stream
His sweetest song of love's delightful dream.
Those distant sloping hills were green and fair,
Sweet odors wantoned on the very air.
Yon orchard bloomed all pink and white,
Like vernal morning bathed in rosy light.
The milk white box-tree bloomed upon the hill,
At eve the song, "Whip-poor-will! Whip-poor-will!"
Came floating softly on the balmy air,
Lulling all to sleep: sleep that respites care.
But now, alas, those dreamy days are o'er,
The notes of warbling birds are heard no more,
All bloom has vanished, vanished in a day,
The fairest tints have turned to sombre gray.
And now a sullen gloom o'er shadows all
E're nature kindly spreads her snowy pall,
While o'er the tomb she sheds a silent tear
A parting tribute to a dying year.
But from those scenes of ruin and decay
My heart now turned quite sick and sad away:
Though soon a cheering light came stealing o'er me,
And other scenes like visions rose before me.
Thus sunshine, ever follows after storm,
Death's not the end, 'tis but a change of form.
As winter just foreruns the gentle spring,
So sorrow's mission's future joy to bring.
So too with me, my life begun in joy.
'Twas life and hope, a hope without alloy,
But now I tread life's dreary maze alone.

No foot of land, no cot to call my own,
Nor dare I even hope for future bliss
If Nature hath no moral couched in this
Refreshing thought, reviving, cheering, good.
If coming spring revive the tiny bud,
Say why, oh! man, say why so slow to learn?
Why not revive the ashes of the urn?
If not, then life is but a hideous death,
A blot, a crime to him who gave me breath.
Does this poor transient life fulfill the whole?
Is there no realm to satisfy the soul?
Those prisoners in a crumbling house of clay
Our thoughts, released, would gladly soar away,
And in that great unbounded space abroad,
Survey the wondrous works and ways of God .
How sad our case when to our troubled breasts
Hope comes no more most welcome of all guests.
Hath Nature bade us hopeless yearn and sigh,
Or made a want she would not gratify?
Why grope we here, 'twixt doubt and hope so long;
Why choose we right, yet do the grossest wrong?
Why wage we here this vain unequal strife,
If not to rise to higher forms of life?
Are there not lives, like banners, half unfurled,
Barks foundered "freight half given to the world,"
Or like a courier lying dumb and cold,
Some message to an anxious race half told.
Fond friendships like the forest tempest torn,
And riven hearts oft left to bleed and mourn.
Hard lessons, yet, without resultant good,
Ambitions stifled at their very flood,
Oppression sore, and grievous to be borne,
The pomp of wealth, its pride and cruel scorn!
Our humblest claims in life are set aside,
And oh! our sacred trusts how oft betrayed!
Our brightest hours are ever wing'd the fleetest,
And all that's sweet is lost, lost when sweetest.
And we have joys no words have yet revealed,
And woes so deep that e'en our lips are sealed.
Our joys come like the bubbles on a stream,
A moment full, then vanish as a dream.
And there are souls that walk beneath the moon
Whose lives from early morn till highest noon
Are but strange missions here of unmixed sorrow,
Who date their hopes away, some bright to-morrow.
Oh, human bliss, how brief thy longest stay,
Scarce here ere swiftly winged upon thy way
Illusive as a mirage in the sky,
That oft hath charmed the wondering gazer's eye.

Art thou a glimpse, a sweet foretaste of Heaven.
A kind decoy to struggling mortals given?
Oh! tell me what I am, or whence came I,
Or why I live thus doomed to fail and die,
To perish like a burning taper's flame,
My words, my thoughts, my nature and my name.
Do those whose absence makes us bitter weep,
Survive, or sleep, their one eternal sleep?
Beyond this realm of death is there a clime
Where we can balance all the wrongs of time?
Where mothers, wailing o'er the empty chair,
May find their long lost infant treasure there?
Or shall we ever look again on faces
Gone, gone and left us only vacant places.
'Twas by no choice of mine that I exist.
Drawn by a fate no power can resist.
I'm swiftly tending to that dark beyond,
That "Silent Land" whose tenants ne'er respond.
Does Mind result from organs finely wrought,
Or must its hidden source be elsewhere sought?
I have my life in common with the beast,
A better brain, instinct somewhat decreased.
I boast somewhat of reason in its stead.
(But whether of the twain's most wisely led?)
Through life I breathe with him, one common breath,
And in the end I die with him one common death.
Both touched by sorrow, I, deep stained by sin,
Does death end all for him? real life begin
With me?   Is Mind the essence pure of all we see,
The earnest, promise, pledge, Thou Still SHALL BE?
Doth life through endless forms itself renew,
Evolving noblest thoughts to-day in one,
Next in the fleecy cloud or pearly dew?
Perchance a pebble, glistening 'neath the sun.
The lark that wakes the morn his song to sing,
The rill that trickles down the mountain side,
Yea, more, the creeping worm, the humblest thing.
The modest wayside flower, the ocean wide.
Is in a sense my sister or my brother;
The future, all my hope, the past, my mother.
I long for life, away beyond the tomb,
Where thoughts immortal and eternal bloom;
Nor dims the light of that eternal noon,
Where harps and lyres, triumphant songs attune;
Nor doomed to silence while I'm there,
I'll view the picture that I paint while here.
I'll want to know how fares my fellow man:
If perfect life's the goal in nature's plan:
To visit scenes familiar on this stage;

And wistful watch each fruitful passing age.
And then no matter how or where I am,
I'll want to hear good news from Uncle Sam,
The next Centennial year a noble score,
His charge five hundred millions may be more.
And next I'm sure 'twould please me much to find,
This North and South all one in heart and mind.
A ballot full and free, an honest count,
And best of all, no "bloody shirt" to flaunt.
La Belle France still holding on her way,
Beneath her young Republic's gently sway,
Her sons abandoned all their faction hate,
And pushing on the grand old car of state.
Abandored too, that wild Utopian dream,
And onward pushing like a good old team,
In science let great Prussia lead the way,
And Russia too in triumph see her day.
The land of Wallace, Bruce of Bannockburn,
For freedom's cause must take her turn.
Let Erin's question like a cauldron boil,
John Bull go down and Patrick hold the soil.
Let woman take a nobler, better stand,
And with the potent ballot in her hand,
Just wage her well, a good and valliant fight,
Opposing wrong, defending every right.
No more the thoughtless devotee of fashion,
No more the slave to mankind's baser passion;
Deceit in man scarce known up n the earth,
And woman brought to prize good honest worth.
I'll want to know a thousand other things,
To know about the planets, moons and rings,
And other rings not quite so good or great,
That clog the wheels of justice and of state,
To find sweet Freedom's banner wide unfurled.
"On earth, good will to men." Throughout the world,
To find full more of life and less of sorrow,
To find a Golden age, the world's To-morrow.

THE PILOT SHIP.

[Suggested by a picture in Harper's Weekly.]

I see a bark! 'tis night upon the sea,
And the scene suggests a pleasing thought to me.
O'er those gunwales dash the soaring billows,
Upon the deck there stand two stalwart fellows;
Aloft in hand each holds a torch alight.
Each is peering through a glass into the night.
Now these are pilots come to pilot o'er

Some struggling vessel to the ever-nearing shore.
They have left a city where the mansions bright
And the streets are all aglow with life and light.
We have asked a question—asked it long ago—
And the answer how we long and strive to know !
When the tyrant Death in chains hath bound us,
And our friends are weeping anxious round us :
When the last fond signal's fondly given,
And the golden bowl's in sunder riven,
When all of life for us is done and o'er,
Will the pilots come to meet us—meet us from the mystic shore ?

I'LL NO REGRET MY NANNIE, O.

THE ITHER SIDE 'O IT.

I TOOK a paper up and there I read,
  In plainest black and white, my Nannie wed :
Sic news did gar my head all dizzy, O,
And rushing thoughts did keep me busy, O.

And then I thought, I'm no much worse, if any, O,
Then most guid men who lose Nannie, O :
The cause of loss I cannot gather, O,
I'll only dust around and find anither, O.

There's sure anither just as kind and canny, O,
For this world was never short a Nannie, O :
If she was false I'm better clear o' her,
A fickle wife, I've aye had fear o' her.

There's sure some guid amang the many, O,
Why stop to greet the loss of Nannie, O :
This life is just one battle fierce and strang,
How noble he who rather bears than wrang.

'Tis all in bearing that true manhood's shown,
For oft our hearts are left to bleed alone,
To face our foes, nor yield to any, O,
'Tis oft a good man's luck to lose his Nannie, O.

CHORUS.

Then never while your living currents flow
Should you regret a faithless Nannie, O :
I vow I'll not regret a Nannie, O,
I swear I'll not regret a Nannie, O.

ELEGIAC POEM.

NOW henceforth, sacred to the dead,
  To those who bitter weep and mourn,
Or those who weary hither tread,
  To rest here in appointed turn

Alike, the breath of flow'ry May,
  To them, alike the winter's gloom,
Alike, the dull cold autumn day,
  No change disturbs the silent tomb.

Here rank and cast are laid aside,
  The cotter's like the millionaire :
The *motives* of our lives are tried,
  Nor bribes, the least, avail us here.

Here, slumb'ring in his lowly bed,
  While seasons endless come and go,
Shall rest the aged Pilgrim's head,
  Through summer's heat and winter's snow.

He, in this land of shadows dim,
  Of sightless eyes and organs dumb,
His sons unknown, unthought by him,
  To rank and short-lived honors come.

And here shall sleep the babe, new born,
  The stalwart man, in prime of life,
The loved one from the lover torn,
  The husband and the fait ful wife.

The prattling child, the household's pride,
  Its light and joy, its fairest flower,
To this dark bourne must turn aside,
  Low laid in death's untimely hour.

And youth enwrapped in Hope's fond dream,
  (The nectar in the blighted flower,
A bubble burst upon the stream),
  Low laid by death's relentless power.

And here shall come the lovely bride,
  Upon her lips, half-uttered vows :
To rest forever by her side,
  Here, too, perchance, shall come her sponse.

Here come the stricken ones to mourn,
  And o'er the tomb lone vigils keep :

The moss-grown slab, the sculptured urn,
  The mournful willow here shall weep.

The murmuring brook beneath the hill,
  The wild bird warbling o'er their bed ;
Sequested here, the whippoorwill
  Shall chant sad requiems for the dead.

A SATIRE ON WOMAN.

B. M. I guess I've guessed the who !
  You say I'm false, you ever true,
But claims like that are naething new,
    A female saint !
Just ask the Deil. He's truthful, too ;
    Without a taint.

You call men monsters ; I say well ;
If words and actions ought can tell,
You like the monsters monstrous well.
    Your like the rest—
All high pretence, and but a sell ;
    A flirt at best.

"Take up thy gauntlet, I'll not try."
You're right. For in the joust you'd die;
But if you should, your sword take I.
    For in the tilt
Your thrusts at me gae harmless by,
    Mine crowd the hilt.

"Deceitful man," ye hae your share then,
And faith, a gay guid when, to spare then
You play it unco weel, that's mare then.
    I tell nae news
Of that ye ken the warl's aware then,
    Gie Diel's their dues.

When mankind treats you squarely O,
Do you reward him fairly O ?
Oh, do you jilt him sairly, O,
    And ca' him daft—
And then repent it early O ?
    I've kenned it aft.

Show me the man o' worth and grace
That finds a lass 'o suit his case,

Or finds that treasure 'mang your race,
        That treasure fair
The " wise man " ranks in highest place—
        A ruby rare.

What honied words she'll tell him :
Wi' witching ways, she'll buy and sell him ;
And then, awa' wi' some poor skellum !
        A victim she,
A fickless buke, in gold and vellum.
        Poor victim he!

While she pursues, 'tis well with him,
But just reversed, his hopes grow dim .
Her head takes up another whim,
        He was too cheap;
When he desponds, her joys at brim :
        She sows, she'll reap.

Suppose twe suitors, you at stake,
True man the one, and one a rake,
Now tell me honest, which you'd take,
        'Side issues equal.
Upon the last I'd millions stake
        And bide the sequel.

You choose mere brass, reject pure gold,
A lie is truth when smoothly told,
Nor dream how cheap yourself is sold,
        Till cast away :
Then comes that tale so often told,
        "You've had your day."

Ye tamper wi' a guilded bait,
'Til prudence speaks, but speaks too late :
The die you've cast, or dared a fate
        Not oft averted
All men are objects of your hate !
        Your love's inverted.

I've often kenned ye get together,
And for twa guide lang hours blather
About some wim wi' ane anither
        Wi' unco zest
That in a scale might tip a feather,
        Just thro at best.

Ye'll clack and cackle o'er a bonnet,
As though the worl' depended on it.

Sole care to buy a dress and don it,
    Nor heed the bill,
Much less the toil and care that won it,
    Through good and ill.

Here on life's stage a part is true,
We " speak our piece," or play it through.
Mankind cajole and " taffy " you :
    'Tis truth I tell.
I show the good and evil, too :
    It's just as well.

Thrice happy for our hapless race,
If e'er it reach that happy case,
When sex on sex dependence place :
    O, rich reward,
When sex to sex less oft proves base
    By deed or word.

While mortals here we're tossed and driven
Our hearts bowed down and sorrow riven,
If e'er there comes a breath from Heaven
    That thrills the soul,
'Tis when that magic touch is given,
    When love makes whole.

Once in the fields of Eden fair,
Unknown a tear ; untouched by care,
Ere woman, thou, or sin cam'st there,
    Wi'thy thrawn brood,
Whose deep laid plots, and schemes unfair
    Supplanted good.

I reigned proud laird, o' bird and brute,
'Till " clooty " showed the cloven cloot,
Then i and thou got " fired out;"
    Thou ken'st fu' well
When sin came there, thou wast the root
    'Twas planned in Hell.

Thy lug to flattery, aye awake,
Thou gossip'dst with a squirming snake,
And di'lst although forbidden, take
    That cursed bait
Then came and blathered like a glake,
    And sealed my fate.

When awfu' wars lay waste the earth,
And famine comes, and dreadful dearth,

Man sore laments that thou had'st birth
Thou root of evil,
Too great the cost for a' thou'st worth,
Thou angel d—l.

But man, what woes the fates allot him,
The thief that robs, the snare that caught him,
The suicide, the " thug," that shot him,
All sums up this :
" A woman somewhere at the bottom."
Here ends his bliss.

Yet man, why at thy lot repine,
Why thus lament this fate of thine :
This solace take, this solace mine
It comforts me,
The bruised grape alone yields wine,
So comfort thee.

POSTSCRIPT.

Now one of two maun always squeal,
So I propose gin ye think weel,
To lend my lance o' burnished steel,
I've ane to spare
It gives a prod that ane can feel,
T'were only fair

[A satire on man was written in reply to this satire on woman, but it was a mere literary jumble, consequently could not be published.

There are two sides to every question. Man and woman are perhaps equally to blame for the difficulties that exist between them, and there is no hope of a better state of affairs until the race has risen to a higher plane of moral integrity.]

SOME THINGS SAD TO SEE.

A MAIDEN blighted in her love ;
Strong manhood stricken in its prime :
A hawk pounce down upon a dove ;
A child born 'ere its proper time ;
A sweet flower blighted in a day :
A bright life end midst clouds and gloom ;
A romping child forbid to play :
Infirm old age without a home.

THE BONNIE BELLES O' BRADFORD.

*T*HEY look so sweet, 'tis complete for one to meet.
 No matter where those treasures rare, those angels
  fair,
By Heaven sent, so kindly lent, for man's content.
  Those lasses in their teens,
  Those bonnie belles o' Bradford.
  Our lasses i' their teens.

Caressing glances, shy advances, all enhances,
Sweet depend, let man attend and safe defend,
By honest thrift or vengeance swift, this precious gift.
  Our lasses i' their teens,
  The bonnie belles o' Bradford,
  Those lasses i' their teens.

Let all the city heed my ditty, love and pity,
Love and charm, with feeling warm protect from harm,
E'er before them, watching o'er them, still adore them,
  Those lasses in their teens,
  The bonnie belles o' Bradford,
  Our lasses i' their teens.

But let him glower, who 'buses power in passion's hour ;
O'er prison bar, who ever dare their bliss to mar,
Or would decoy, and then destroy that sacred joy,
  A lassie in her teens,
  The bonnie belles o' Bradford,
  Sweet lasses i' their teens.

For well we know ('twas ever so,) that all we owe—
Joys of leisure, fonts of pleasure—is to that treasure,
All so smiling, with them whiling, time beguiling,
  Our lasses i' their teens,
  The bonnie Belles o' Bradford,
  Dear lasses i' their teens.

THE HILLS OF BRADFORD.

I love the bonnie hills of Bradford,
 Beneath those bonnie hills the winding Tuna flows ;
  Around those hills weird shadows fall, and sunlight
   glows
  Upon those bonnie hills of Bradford.

I love the verdant hills of Bradford.
When o'er those verdant hills the tender leaves and
flowers
Bursting from their tombs, and the glory of the vernal
hours
Decks all the verdant hills of Bradford.

I love the blooming hills of Bradford.
When o'er those blooming hills the breath of summer
comes,
When in the woody dells the milk-white box-tree
blooms,
Among the blooming hills of Bradford.

I love the purple hills of Bradford
When o'er those purple hills the purple blends with red,
And when the purple leaf or faded flower has fled
And left the purple hills of Bradford.

I love the snowy hills of Bradford
When all those snowy hills have shed their summer
dress so gay,
And naught is left but leafless trees in sombre gray,
Upon the snowy hills of Bradford.

—

THE PEBBLE IN THE OCEAN.

I stood by the ocean at eve, when the waves were at
rest :
The stars were reflected like studs from its transparent
breast.
A pebble let fall from my hand set a ripple in motion ;
The ripple set acres of waters in gentle commotion.
A heavy gun'd vessel lay anchor'd some distance away,
And it heaved, I know, like the tiniest bark in that bay.
I said that the mind of our race just resembles the
ocean—
The tiniest pebble of thought sets a ripple in motion,
The pebbles will drop and the ocean unceasingly move,
For 'tis by the motion of mind that our race must im-
prove.
Then why should we grieve for those dogmas now pass-
ing away ?
For dogmas like men, must decay when they've lived
out their day.

"WHO SENT THEE TO BLOOM?"

AY, merry robin, who sent thee to sing
  So sweetly thy soul-stirring lay?
Some loved one, no doubt, is near by :
  Then sing, robin, sing, while you may.

When weary of fashion's cold ways,
  When weary of frescoes and paint,
Sham friendships, and all of that sort.
  Conventional folk, and restraint.

Away to the wild woods I fly ;
  Kind nature ne'er spurned me away ;
The song of the robin, so sweet,
  And the posies beguile me to stay.

Say, pretty flower, who sent thee to bloom,
  Away on this hillside so drear?
I find thee neglected, alone :
  What solace can comfort thee here?

Thou seemest not sad in thy life,
  Could mankind afford thee no room,
Receiving thy perfume and smiles?
  To fulfill some mission thou'st come.

We each have some mission to fill ;
  No darkness, where love lights the way ;
We each may be doing some good,
  In life that is fleeting away.

HOPE.

HEN Hope, that lamp so bright, illumes the droop-
      ing mind,
How soon we fling dull care and sorrow all behind.
How all things change beneath her ever cheering beam ;
All things alike, the sadest like the brightest seem.
We brave the rudest blast that treats us illy :
        Our darkness turns to day,
        Our winters flee away
And spring returns with verdant leaf and snow-white
      lily.

But once let Hope withhold from us her cheering beam,
All things alike, the brightest like the saddest seem
Alike to us, the wailing pine. the weeping willow,
The trilling lark, the skipping lamb, the skimming
    swallow.
We bend beneath the slightest blast that treat us illy ;
      Our sunlight's fled and gone.
      Our buds and blossoms flown
No spring for us, with verdant leaf and snow-white lily.

Then give us hope, that lamp so bright, to cheer the
    mind,
We'll fling our cares and sorrows all behind.
All things are good, the saddest like the brighest seem
When Hope inspires us with her cheering beam,
We'll brave the wintry blasts that treats us illy
      'Till darkness turns to day,
      'Till winter's fled away
And spring returns with verdant leaf and snow-white
    lily.

NEWSBOY'S CHRISTMAS AND NEW YEAR'S

GREETING.

NOW kind friends I would gladly greet you all,
    In my Christmas round, and my New Year's
    call,
But I need not tell, for you knew it before,
How I've toiled to bring all the news to your door.

At the early dawn, 'neath a starry sky,
When the wind blew cold, and the drifts swept by.
Though I often " made," I was sometimes " stuck,"
But I pushed right on, never " blamed my luck."

May we often meet, as we oft have met :
As the years glide past—a hope for us yet ;
In the bright New Year, so soon to come, ·
May no shadow fall on your happy home.

I will hang up my sock near my bedroom door
And the reindeer man, from his wond'rous store,
Will remember me and be kind to you ;
Through the year I remain your newsboy true.

NEWSBOYS' GREETING.

TWELVE months ago since this old year began,
  And I start in the battle of life anew.
  For I feel, what I hope, to be true,
That I'm one year more, the more of a man.

Now I've brought you the news from countries afar,
  And I've brought you the news from countries near,
  Of the "boom" in oil, and the market's scare,
And of earthquakes great, and the clouds of war.

Then of cruel wars 'mong the "bulls" and the "bears,"
  Of the trusting lamb, who ventured in "ille,"
  How he dropped his head, when he dropped his "pile."
Weary ones shuffling this life and its cares.

Towns laid waste by the scourge of fire and wind,
  Then how some bummer was pulled by the cops,
  Next of weddings so bright, and high-toned hops
Of that *bomber* abroad, the "Dynamite Fiend."

But, let me tell you what's better than all,
  'Tis not so much after all, the New Year,
  But the long looked-for Christmas is here
And I think Kris Kringle will give me a call.

So I'll give you my wish, Merry Christmas cheer,
  To my friends every one, to my patrons all,
  Who buy on the street or the homes where I call,
May your lives grow bright, through the whole New Year.

SMILING THROUGH OUR TEARS.

GAILY tripping like a little sprite,
  Airy motions, graceful form, face so bright,
Thus I met a little maiden fair,
Light of heart and free from every care.

How my heart went out to wish her well,
When, poor thing, she, tripping lightly by, fell,
Looked then at me, smiling through her tears,
More than lovely in her tender years.

Smooth I stroked and pressed her little head,
Laughing now, light away she fled,
And I stood there musing so intent,
For no words could give my feelings vent.

How we yearn for childhood's laughing years!
For its smiles to mingle with our tears.
Smiles and joys, alas! long fled away,
Smiles have fled and tears now long delay.

Buoyant youth, now slow to think or learn!
Oft between the cradle and the urn
Pass we sadly through the fleeting years,
Happy if found smiling through our tears.

THE BELLES OF BRADFORD.

[In reply to the "Belles of Bradford," by B. J. B.]

I WOULD not pass the belles of Bradford
Should smiling beauty be my game—oh, no!
And if from home love-making I shall ever go,
The most ravishing eyes
I know under the skies
Will tempt me to set out for Bradford.

I would not slight the Belles of Bradford
For those vile rubber boots which, in their care
For their excellent health, I see them wear.
And they can't be beat,
In the matter of feet,
In old Oildom, the belles of Bradford.

Let others chide the belles of Bradford
For their hoydenish skirts and all of that;
To me they look ang   e n that Derby hat,
Which I hated the m   o
I had seen it, before
I saw the jaunty thing in Bradford.

Warm are their hearts, the belles of Bradford,
And firm the limbs with which, early and late
These muddy thoroughfares called streets they 'navigate.'
And for them 'tis but fun
The streetcars to outrun,
For "walkists" are the belles of Bradford.

A wide berth give the belles of Bradford,
A bashful young man if you are, and can't
Find in your native town the blushing prude you want.
But if you want a wife
That will last you for life,
You'll find that precious " rib " in Bradford.

—A. B. Feale.

FAREWELL TO THE TUNA.

FAREWELL to the beautiful Tuna
For now I must go.
No more shall I stroll on those hillsides
In sadness alone,
Or list to the streamlets that murmur
So sweetly below.

Farewell to those hillsides, now burnished
With purple and gold.
Farewell to those scenes that I've cherished
So fondly and long ;
Those scenes that have yielded me pastimes
And pleasures untold.
How often they've turned all my sadness
To pleasure and song.

Farewell to those scenes my solace
And comfort in sorrow,
How oft will I call them to mind,
When I'm far, far away,
For often they've taught me to hope
For a brighter to-morrow.
And bid me forget all my sadness
And sorrow to-day.

Farewell to the robin that awakened
The Spring's early morn ;
Farewell to the pheasant and squirrel,
The blackbird so gay,
Why robbed am I thus of your music
So merry in May.

THE EVOLUTION OF TEMPERANCE.

I HAVE watched this temperance question long
Though I've nothing really strange or new :
I would have my little say in song,
    Ever careful only for the true.

I have heard the Murphys and the Goughs,
    McConnells and the smaller fry,
Heard the whiskey dealer's cruel scoff,
    And I've heard the wounded orphan's cry.

We have plotted, planned and oft devised
    Prohibition, option, moral suasion,
Legislated, legal statutes oft revised,
    But the common fruit was law's evasion.

Surely there's a medium in all things,
    And a certain point on either side,
Hail the healthful moral that this sings,
    Whereon rectitude can not abide.

We have good and evil for the choosing,
    And some giant evils must exist ;
He alone's the hero, who refusing
    Steadfast, all allurement doth resist.

Midst clouds and smoke and cannon's rattle,
    Good and evil war to win the day,
Every hero's born of strife and battle,
    Strength he gains in every fiery fray.

Nature holds a crown for those who strive,
    Strive's her mandate, strive my child or die ;
For the fittest must and shall survive,
    Nothing in my realm e'er may idle lie.

Go then drunkards drink your fill,
    Fill your poisoned goblets to the brim,
That is best for you which quickly kills,
    Craze your brain and palsey every limb.

Only death you seek, only death you'll find,
    Nature's laws are vindicated when
When in mercy she eradicates your kind
    And your place is filled with nobler men.

[This poem was written many years ago. At the
present time I would hesitate to endorse it's sentiments.
We should help the fallen. I have seen the drunkard
reform and become a good man.   AUTHOR.]

THE ORPHAN'S PLEA.

OH, please don't say you're not my mother,
    'Twill seem so good to little me :
Then your Willie will be my little brother,
'Twill be more cheery, like it used 'o be.
I used to have a mother all my own,
I 'member well the morning that she died,

And left her little Mary all alone,
And papa looked so sad, brother Willie cried.
And when I heard them say that she was dead,
I went and laid my hand upon her brow ;
My heart was filled with grief and dread,
'Twas dreadful cold, I think I feel it now.
They put her down, way down, deep in the ground ;
(I think some day she'll get alive again :)
They laid the earth and sods up all around,
We put some flowers around her head and then
Poor Willie and my papa they died too,
And they are lying by my mamma's side :
So now I have no mother left but you,
You'll never know how hard I've tried and tried
To think your Willie is my little brother ;
Now can't you take poor Mary for your own ?
Do tell me then that you will be my mother.
Just think that I'm your little Mary Doan ;
I'll try and think my mother is not dead,
And when the Winter's gone and Spring is here,
I'll plant some posies 'round her head.
I think she'd like to have some posies there,
But tell me, won't you be my mother?

AN IDYL.

I MET her in the vernal dream,
Beside a rippling sun-lit stream,
When swallows built with mud and leaves
Beneath the ancient mossy eaves,
And blackbirds carolled wild and free
Midst rustling leaves from tree to tree.
Close by their cozy nests, new made,
Nearby upon the soggy glade,
The redbreast chanted in his glee ;
And yet the sweetest voice to me,
Was hers, that lass my only shrine,
That bonnie, bonnie lass o' mine.

I saw her in the morning hours,
Reclined beneath the leafy bowers,
Where birdies sang, and humming bees
Made music 'mong the budding trees,
And sipped sweet nectar from the flowers
'Twas in those early morning hours,
A myriad of pearly dewdrops bright,
Were sparkling in the rosy light,

Which bathed in joy the rolling lea ;
And yet the brightest far to me
Was she, sweet lass, my only shrine,
That bonnie, bonnie lass o 'mine.

I saw her in the Summer's 'een,
When all the fields were clothed in green
A rainbow hung upon the sky,
All beauteous to the ravished eye,
And odors " wantoned round the vine,"
'Twas Nature's sacred shrine,
A place where gods and genii dwell,
No human faltering tongue can tell,
The wonderous beauty of that place,
No gods nor fabled genii's face,
Was e'en so sweet as hers, my shrine,
That bonnie, bonnie lass o' mine.

Oh, then ye powers supreme, divine,
The gracious will be wholly thine,
So give me her in humblest cot
If happily thus I'd envy not
The greatest earthly prince his power,
Or regnant queen her richest dower,
Nor heed Dame Fortune's smile or frown,
To simply call that lass my own,
Not all the priceless rubies rare
Not all of India's treasures fair
Would I accept for her, my shrine,
That bonnie, bonnie lass o' mine.

I'LL NE'ER FORGET MY NANNIE, O.

O' a' the bonnie lassies e'er I met,
  There's nane like Nannie yet :
She's aye sae gentle kind and cannie, O,
This world has not anither Nannie, O.

CHORUS.

So never while my living currents flow, ·
Can I forget my gentle Nannie, O ;
I vow I'll not forget my Nannie, O,
I swear I'll not forget my Nannie, O.

Her neat-kept raven hair looks aye sae weel,
(I think this banging hair just bangs the de'il).
Her shoulders slope, her waist's fu' slender, O.
Her e'e is dark, her voice fu' tender, O.

Her rosy cheek, her brow's like driven snee,
And Heaven beams frae out her deep dark e'e :
Her voice is like the cooing o' a dove,
She's sic a lass nae *man* could help but love.

Ah! many lang, lanely hours hae fled
Sin' last I look'd upon her bonnie head,
Or baskit neath the glances o' her e'e,
And oh ! how lang and lane those hours to me.

Oh, speed the days and pass the hours o'er,
And let me hear her gentle voice once more.
Since last I saw my gentle Nannie, O,
The woods and fields hae bloom'd all bonnie, O.

The fragrant flowers hae bloom'd o'er hill and dale,
And singing birds hae wing'd o'er mount and vale :
But now, alas ! those singing birds are fled,
And all the simmer's bloom is pale and dead.

Yet soon I'll gie the Fates a sudden slip,
To me 'twill only be a pleasant trip,
To hie awa' and see my Nannie, O.
She has my heart, she has my hand for weal or woe.

One potent cause for all our grief and woe
Is this, that men neglect their Nannie, O;
Who trifles finds transgressors rue the day,
Then, men, do what you will when you're away.

But by the holy powers above you,
By all the hopes of those that love you,
Unless you court a life of grief and woe,
Then don't, oh, don't neglect your Nannie, O.

RATHER POINTED AGAIN.

A LADY ANSWERS THE WRITER OF THE AUTOGRAPH ALBUM

Editor Sunday News :

The following appeared in your last Sunday's issue.
Will you kindly oblige me by publishing an answer to it?

RATHER POINTED.

A young lady of this city asked a gentleman acquaint-

ance to write something in her autograph album. He
complied, and this is the way he did it :

Oh ! happy is the man that can
    A woman's impish arts defy.
You may not think that I'm that man,
    And yet that very man am I.
Another thing is just as true—
My words do not apply to you.

THE REPLY.

A woman's impish arts indeed !
    Pray tell me true, sir, if you can,
How often woman is deceived
    By that deceitful monster man ?

That very man you say are you—
    Who can a woman's arts defy.
Conceited man, though dost not know :
    Take up thy gauntlet ; I'll not try.

Per force, per se, I say to thee :
    " My words to you may not apply ; "
Untrue are thou, oh ! B. J. B.,
    Whilst ever true, B. M am I.

SING, OH, SING THAT SONG FOR ME AGAIN.

SING, oh sing that song for me again,
    It whispers thoughts so sweet to me of yore :
Of many things I dream that happened then
    Of dearly loved ones only gone before.

Yes, sing ! oh, sing ! for me again,
    It tells of happy childhood's hopes and fears :
Like strains of music from some far-off shore ;
    It comes down the mystic stream of years.

As o'er tempestuous seas we've cheerless sailed,
    Through dreary days and nights we've come ;
What bursts of joy when some lone vessel's hailed,
    Perchance a sail or craft we've known at home.

" A sail !" then " ship ahoy!" and "whither bound !"
    Each bosom heaves—and tides of life run high ;
While from those passing decks we hear resound,
    A burst of joy—now sparkles every eye.

And so in life, when o'er its troubled sea,
   For weary months and years we've cheerless gone:
Perchance a word or act of childish glee,
   Recalls some joyous scene that once we've known

Then sing, oh, sing that song for me once more,
   It tells of happy childhood's joys and dreams :
In it I seem to live my childhood o'er,
   And sweet, oh, sweet, the fond illusion seems.

ACROSTIC.

(By a highly-esteemed lady friend.)

In Memorium.

JESUS said unto him, " thou shalt love the Lord thy God, with all thy heart, and with all thy soul, and with all thy mind

AND the peace of God, which passeth all understanding, shall keep your hearts and minds through Christ Jesus.

MAKE us glad according to the days wherein thou hast afflicted us, and the years wherein we have seen evil.

EVEN as the son of man came not to be ministered unto, but to minister, and to give his life a ransom for many.

SAY not ye, there are yet four months and then cometh harvest, behold, I say unto you, lift up your eyes and look on the fields for they are white already to harvest.

BEHOLD the lamb of God that taketh away the sins of the world.

EVEN the righteousness of God, which is by faith in Jesus Christ unto all, and upon all them that believe for there is no difference.

RETURN unto me and I will return unto you, saith the Lord of Hosts.

NAY in all these things we are more than conquerors through him that loved us.

EVEN Christ pleased not himself.

YE are bought with a price, be not ye the servants of men.

Brief Sayings.

Brief Sayings.

We often diet in order to live it.

The day laborer has that which is often denied to Kings and Emperors—a good appetite and refreshing sleep.

The grandest spectacle on earth is the man who stands up like a tower of strength in the midst of his own ruins.

Man is so constituted that even a smile or a word of friendly recognition enables him to bear up under the most grievious burdens.

There is that which seems to exalt a man when it is debasing him, and there is that which seems to debase him when it is exalting him.

Our progress as a race is like that of a man who had lived through all generations profiting by his own experience and that of his fellows.

The grape must be bruised before it will yield its wine, and so of the human mind—it must be bruised in the wine press of the bitterest experiences before it will yield its richest thought.

Woman is a strange mixture of divine goodness and human cussedness.

Knowledge is not subject to that law of arithmetic which applies to our other possessions ; it increases in proportion to the amount we impart to others.

The loveliest flowers are those of domestic felicity, but like other domestic flowers, they come not as a spontaneous growth, but live and thrive only by the utmost care and attention.

The majority of heroes are unwritten. We often diet in order to live it.

If Life had no struggles it would have no triumphs.

Universal brotherhood admits of no creed but brotherhood.

Little men boast, great men are above it.

The penalty for expressing an honest opinion is very light now—ostracism, that's all.

Never despair of finding a lady in a cabin, or too confident of finding one in a mansion.

We know things best by contrast. To know joy at greatest heights we must have known sorrow at its greatest depths.

It is an irrevocable law of Nature that the scales of Justice must balance sometime, somewhere, somehow.

The most reliable resolutions are those made in the presence of the greatest temptations.

To every life there should be a Pisga's top and a Promised Land. Every life has its Gethsemana, but for every Gethsemane there is a mount of transfiguration.

A coquette is a woman without any heart, who makes a fool of a man without any head.

Of the two, I would rather associate with a man who swears and means no harm, than with a man who prays and means no good.

The minister may pronounce the ceremony, but he cannot marry the couple. Nature only can do that if it is ever done.

It is the very paradox of thought that he only who can dive the deepest in thought will be capable of the loftiest flights of thought.

The natural man is the only true man. Posthumous honors avail nothing to the dead.

Human progress makes the crowned heads of the world only refugees.

Necessity is a goal that drives us to greater effort.

If I am immortal, so is my dog; and I don't deny either.

To judge a man justly we must understand his case from first to last.

Locks and keys are the ever-present proofs of human depravity.

A man without faults could scarcely be a popular man. We must have something in common with our fellow-men to be able to sympathize with them and to be appreciated by them in return. A great philosopher says: "I have committed every known fault." A life without battles is a life without victory.

A tender heart with a hard head makes a model man ; but a hard heart and a hard head makes a bad combination.

Good whiskey—that which kills the quickest.

There is a threadbare coat in store for the man of independent thought.

A bad government is a political volcano. Loyalty is the result of good government.

We often miss the truth by thinking we have it.

The greater the truth the slower we are to learn it.

Man is by Nature the sole proprietor of his own mind.

You can do no good for a man if there be no good in him.

The monkeys are the only party really injured by Darwin's theory.

Those who produce the wealth of a country, enjoy the least of their labor.

I may see visions, but my neighbor is not bound to believe my report of them.

We receive a man for what there is on him, and retain him for what there is in him.

Hunger and want are grim realities, but they are more tolerable than so-called charity.

Happiness is like a mirage or a will o' the wisp, ever luring us on, till, as a child, wearied with its toys, we lay us down in the sleep of oblivion.

Death is a great reformer.

Flattery is a first-class power.

There is a gospel in soap and water.

Man proposes, but woman disposes.

Before we have learned to live, we die.

The witness that needs to be sworn is by nature a false witness.

Never let your hand go where your heart cannot go.

He who is just to himself can be just to others.

Genius is often mistaken for insanity, and vice versa.

Treat all good thoughts as guests, and bad thoughts as intruders.

An epigram is a stuffed club.

Man knows the least of himself.

The tailor makes a large proportion of men.

A few words will often express a great thought.

Some people mistake indigestion for religion.

We make money the only end of our existence: it should be only the means to a good end.

Dancing is the poetry of motion; music is the poetry of the mind.

Nature is a slowly unfolding revelation, and all other revelations must abide by her final decisions.

All I know of the future may be written in three words—I don't know.

A frivolous woman worships the man that ruins her, and ruins the man that worships her.

We can see everything but ourselves

A logical woman and a crowing hen are rare exceptions. Her conclusions are intuitive.

Nature produces by wholesale and retains by retail.

Vice performs all the duties of judge, jury and hangman.

All men are not born equal, but all men have equal rights before the law.

Lying actions are no better than lying words.

What we fail to decide for ourselves others will decide for us.

To disbelieve after proof is as stupid as to believe without proof.

In our true calling we see no drudgery. Out of it, all is drudgery.

Seek praise and the world will deny you the credit which is justly your due.

At twenty we think ourselves superior to our fathers and mothers. At forty we often respect our inferiority.

The miracle of Balaam's ass presents no difficulties to me. It is nothing uncommon for an ass to speak.

If the bears were commissioned to devour all the disobedient children, they would fall behind in their orders

Men do not like to believe in their ape origin, and yet nine-tenths of them are not ashamed to act the ape.

The schoolmaster cultivates the back, the scholar cultivates his head, and the dancing master cultivates his heels, which is the secret of the latter's great popularity.

The best help to give the needy is something to do.

Truth needs not a body-guard. Error only needs defense.

I have seen preachers with very fine deliveries who had nothing to deliver.

Experience is the raw material wherewith the wise make proverbs.

An old bacheler is one who has missed the chance of making some woman miserable.

Every man and woman that is born into the world has a natural right to live in this world until they prove an enemy to their kind.

If there be a spark of good in the liquor traffic it must survive, if not, it must go down because of its own corruptions.

" Whatsoever ye would that men should do under you, do ye so even unto them," is the only creed the world ever needed.

Man is the mysterious product of vast ages, waking up to the reality of his own individual existence and the wonders around him, but he knows not whence he came, or whither he goes. His body is from the earth, but that is as nothing compared to the whole man. What of the *I* or the *me* that takes knowledge of his own individuality and that of others, and the wonderful relationship of things that surround him.

Two things I've found beneath the sun. Yea, more— there are no less than three that serve us mortal men alike : The empty honors of the world, our shadows, and that ever-charming creature, woman. When we in eager haste pursue, they flee, and when we flee they eagerly pursue.

To live ! What do these words at least imply ?
But this—to all around some pleasure give ;
So scatter seeds of kindness while we live,
To grow and blossom, blossom when we die.

Dictionaries do not make facts.

Pity and contempt are half sisters.

An old bachelor is a noun, neuter genter, third person singular, and agrees with nothing expressed or understood.

The human family is divided into two classes : Those who worry because they are not married, and those who worry because they are married.

Bigotry is the first born of ignorance.

A good husband and a good wife are a rare team.

The only true aristocracy is that of the head and heart.

The greatest discovery—a man ; the luckiest find—a woman.

Was the healing of Peter's mother-in-law a blessing to Peter ?

Dogs are sometimes more human than their masters.

It is better to oppress one's self than suffer the least restriction by others.

Love is an unutterable goneness as it were.

We miss the sun when it is under a cloud, friends when they are absent, and health when we are sick.

Wages are often so high one cannot reach them.

Inability in the pulpit can only thrive by gullability in the pew.

We may be robbed of our reputation, but never of our character, without our own consent.

Happiness consists, not in the abundance of things we possess, but in the simplicity of our wants.

It is one thing to *train* the mind ; it is another thing to *educate* the mind.

Man must have traveled far up in the path of evolution before he could tell lies, and he will have to travel a long ways further before he will stop telling lies.

There are three stages in every useful life. First, we are apprentices wherein we learn the use of tools. Next, we go out as journeymen to learn that there are often many ways of accomplishing the same purpose. But not until our false conceits are all tamed down, are worthy of masterhood, or to be called masters.

Selected Gems.

FALLEN.

[This poem was written by a lost woman while in Detroit jail. It is sad to think that one so intellectually gifted should be brought thus low. Aside from the sympathetic chords which it will touch in every heart, it is meritorious as a literary work.]

The iron voice from yonder spire has hushed its hollow
    tone,
And midnight finds me lying here all silent and alone ;
The still moon thro' my window sheds its soft light on
    the floor,
With a melancholy paleness I have never seen before.
And the summer wind comes to me with its sad Æolian
    lay,
As if burthened with the sorrows of a weary, weary day;
Yet the moonlight cannot soothe me of the sickness here
    within,
And the sad wind takes no portion from the bosom's
    weight of sin.

Yet my heart and all its pulses seem so quietly to rest,
That I scarcely feel them beating in my arms or in my
    breast ;
And these rounded limbs are resting now so still upon
    the bed,
That one would think to see me here that I was lying
    dead.
What if 'twere so ? What if I died—died as I am lying
    now,
With something like to virtue's calm upon this marble
    brow ?
What if I died to-night? Ah! now this slothful heart
    begins to beat,
A fallen wretch like me to pass from earth is sadly sweet.

Yet am I calm—as calm as clouds that slowly float and
    form,
To give their tearful strength to some unpitying summer
    storm ;
As calm as great Sahara, ere the simoon sweeps its waste,
Or as the wide sea, ere the breaking waves its shores
    have laced.
Still, still I have no tears to shed ; these eyelids have no
    store—
The fountain once within me is a fountain now no more.

The moon alone weeps for me now, the pale and thought-
ful moon,
She weeps for dying Mary, through all the night's sweet
noon.
What if I died to-night within these wretched, gilded
walls,
Upon whose crimson length no eye of virtue ever falls?
What would its soulless inmates do when they should
find me here,
With cheek too white for passion's smile, too cold for
passion's tear?
Oh! would one come, and from these arms unclasp the
bauble bands;
Another wrench the jewels off my fairer, whiter hands;
This splendid robe another's form would grace, oh! long
before
The glistening moonlight came again to sleep upon the
floor.

And when they laid me down in earth where pauper's
graves are made,
Beneath no bending weeping willow's angel-haunted
shade,
Who'd come and plant a flower o'er poor Mary's friend-
less grave,
Or trim the tangled wild grass that no summer's wind
could wave?
Who'd raise a stone to mark it from the ruder graves
around,
That the passing stranger's footsteps might respect the
spot of ground?
No stone would stand above me, no little waving tree,
No hand would plant a flower o'er a fallen wretch like
me.

What if I died to-night? And when to-morrow's sun
had crept
What late the softly radiant moon in virgin heaven
slept,
They'd come and find me here. Oh! who would weep
to see me dead?
Who'd bend the knee of sorrow by the pulseless wanton's
bed?
There's one would come—my mother! God bless the
angel's band
That bore her, ere her daughter fell, to yonder quiet land.
Thank God for all the anthems that the gladdened
angels sung
When my mother went to heaven, and I was pure and
young.

I'm all alone to night.   How strange that I should be
  alone !
This splendid chamber seems to want some roue's wonted
  tone.
Yon soulless mirror, with its smooth and all unvarnished
  face,
Sees not these jeweled arms to-night in their unchaste
  embrace.
Oh ! I have fled the fever of that heated, crowded hall,
Where I might claim the richest and gayest of them all—
Where I could smile upon them with that easy, wanton
  grace
That checks the blood of virtue that would struggle in
  my face.

But I hate them all, I scorn them, as they scorn me on
  the street :
I could spurn away the pressure that my lips so often
  meet ;
I could trample on the lucre that their passion never
  spares,
For they've robbed me of a heritage above the price of
  theirs ;
They can never give me back what I have thrown away,
The brightest jewel woman wears througeout her little
  day :
The brightest and the only one, that from the cluster
  riven
Shuts out forever woman's heart from all its hopes of
  heaven.

What if I died to-night—and died as I am lying here ?
There's many a green leaf withers ere the autumn comes
  to sear.
There's many a dew-drop shaken down ere yet the sun-
  shine came,
And many a spark hath died before it wakened into
  flame.
What if I died to-night and left these wretched bonds of
  clay,
To seek beyond this hollow sphere a brighter, better day?
What if my soul passed out and sought that haven of
  the blest
"Where the wicked cease from troubling and the weary
  are at rest ? "

Would angels call me from above, and beckon me to
  come
And join them in their holy songs in that eternal home ?

Would they clasp their hands in gladness when they saw
   my soul set free,
And point beside my mother to a place reserved for me ?
Would they meet me as a sister—as one of precious
   worth,
Who had won a place in heaven by her holiness on earth?
O God ! I would not have my soul go out upon the air,
With all its weight of wretchedness, to wander where?
   oh where?

THANATOPSIS.

To him who, in the love of Nature holds
  Communion with her visible forms, she speaks
A various language : for his gayer hours
She has a voice of gladness and a smile
And eloquence of beauty ; and she glides
Into his darker musings with a mild
And gentle sympathy, that steals away
Their sharpness ere he is aware. When thoughts
Of the last bitter hour come like a blight
Over thy spirit, and sad images
Of the stern agony, and shroud and pall,
And breathless darkness, and the narrow house,
Make thee to shudder and grow sick at heart ;
Go forth under the open sky and list
To Nature's teachings, while from all around—
Earth and her waters, and the depths of air—
Comes a still voice—Yet a few days, and thee
The all-beholding sun shall see no more
In all his course ; nor yet in the cold ground,
Where thy pale form was laid, with many tears,
Nor in the embrace of ocean, shall exist
Thy image. Earth, that nourished thee, shall claim
Thy growth, to be resolved to earth again :
And, lost each human tryce, surrendering up
Thine individual being, shalt thou go
To mix forever with the elements ;
To be a brother to the insensible rock,
And to the sluggish clod, which the rude swain
Turns with his share, and treads upon. The oak
Shall send his roots abroad, and pierce thy mould
Yet not to thine eternal resting-place
Shalt thou retire alone—nor couldst thou wish
Couch more magnificent. Thou shalt lie down
With patriarchs of the infant world,—with kings
The powerful of the earth,—the wise, the good,

Fair forms, and hoary seers of ages past,
All in one mighty sepulchre. The hills,
Rock-ribbed, and ancient as the sun ; the vales
Stretching in pensive quietness between ;
The venerable woods ; rivers that move
In majesty, and the complaining brooks,
That make the meadows green ; and, poured round all,
Old ocean's gray and melancholy waste—
Are but the solemn decorations all
Of the great tomb of man ! The golden sun,
The planets, all the infinite host of heaven,
Are shining on the sad abodes of death,
Through the still lapse of ages. All that tread
The globe are but a handful to the tribes
That slumber in its bosom. Take the wings
Of morning, traverse Barca's desert sands,
Or lose thyself in the continuous woods
Where rolls the Oregon, and hears no sound
Save his own dashings—Yet the dead are there !
And millions in those solitudes, since first
The flight of years began, have laid them down
In their last sleep,—the dead reign there alone !
So shalt thou rest ; and what if thou withdraw
In silence from the living, and no friend
Take note of thy departure? The gay will laugh
When thou art gone, the solemn brood of care
Plod on, and each one, as before, will chase
His favorite phantom ; yet all these shall leave
Their mirth and their employments, and shall come
And make their bed with thee. As the long train
Of ages glide away, the sons of men—
The youth in life's green spring, and he who goes
In the full strength of years, matron and maid,
The bowed with age, the infant in the smiles
And beauty of its innocent age cut off—
Shall one by one, be gathered to thy side
By those who in their turn shall follow them.
So live that when thy summons comes to join
The innumerable caravan that moves
To the pale realms of shade, where each shall take
His chamber in the silent halls of death,
Then go not, like the quarry-slave at night,
Scourged to his dungeon, but, sustained and soothed
By an unfaltering trust, approach thy grave
Like one who wraps the drapery of his couch
About him, and lies down to pleasant dreams.
                                        —William Cullen Bryant.

NEW YEAR'S EVE.

RING out wild bells, to the wild sky,
  The flying cloud, the frosty light ;
  The year is dying in the night ;
Ring out wild bells and let him die.

Ring out the old, ring in the new :
  Ring happy bells, across the snow ;
  The year is going, let him go :
Ring out the false, ring in the true.

Ring out the grief that saps the mind,
  For those that here we see no more ;
  Ring out the feud of rich and poor,
Ring in redress to all mankind.

Ring out a slowly dying cause,
  And ancient forms of party strife :
  Ring in the nobler modes of life,
With sweeter manners, purer laws.

Ring out false pride in place and blood,
  The civic slander and the spite :
  Ring in the lover of truth and right.
Ring in the common love of good.

Ring out old shapes of foul disease,
  Ring out the narrowing lust of gold ;
  Ring out the thousand wars of old,
Ring in the thousand years of peace.

Ring in the valiant man and free,
  The larger heart, the kindlier hand ;
  Ring out the darkness of the land ;
Ring in the Christ that is to be.
                              —*Alfred Tennyson.*

"BLESSED ARE THEY THAT MOURN."

DEEM not they are blest alone
  Whose lives a peaceful tenor keep :
The Power who pities man has shown
  A blessing for the eyes that weep.

The light of smiles shall fill again
  The lids that overflow with tears ;
And weary hours of woe and pain
  Are promises of happier years.

There is a day of sunny rest
  For every dark and troubled night :
And grief may bide an evening guest,
  But joy shall come with early light.

And thou, who, o'er thy friend's low bier,
  Sheddest the bitter drops like rain,
Hope that a brighter, happier sphere
  Will give him to thy arms again.

Nor let the good man's trust depart,
  Though life its common gifts deny—
Though with a pierced and bleeding heart,
  And spurned of men, he goes to die.

For God hath marked each sorrowing day,
  And numbered every secret tear,
And heaven's long age of bliss shall pay
  For all his children suffer here.

THE RIVER TIME.

H ! a wonderful stream is the river Time,
  As it runs through the realm of tears,
With a faultless rhythm and a musical rhyme
And a broader sweep and a surge sublime,
  As it blends in the ocean of years !

How the winters are drifting like flakes of snow,
  And the summers like birds between,
And the years in the sheaf, how they come and they go
On the river's breast with its ebb and its flow,
  As it glides in the shadow and sheen !

There's a magical isle up the river Time,
  Where the softest of airs are playing,
There's a cloudless sky and a tropical clime,
And a song as sweet as a vesper chime,
  And the Junes with the roses are straying.

And the name of this isle is the "Long Ago,"
  And we bury our treasures there :
There are brows of beauty and bosoms of snow,
There are heaps of dust—oh! we loved them so—
  There are trinkets and tresses of hair.

There are fragments of songs that nobody sings,
   There are parts of an infant's prayer,
There's a lute unswept and a harp without strings,
There are broken vows and pieces of rings,
   And the garments our loved used to wear.

There are hands that are waved when the fairy shore
   By the fitful mirage is lifted in air,
And we sometimes hear through the turbulent roar
Sweet voices we heard in the days gone before,
   When the wind down the river was fair.

Oh! remembered for aye be that blessed isle,
   All the day of our life until night:
And when evening glows with its beautiful smile,
And our eyes are closing in slumbers awhile
   May the greenwood of soul be in sight.
        —*Benjamin F. Taylor.*

YOU PUT NO FLOWERS ON PAPA'S GRAVE.

WITH sable-draped banners, and slow measured
   tread,
The flower-laden ranks pass the gates of the dead:
And seeking each mound where a comrade's form rests,
Leave tear-bedewed garlands to bloom on his breast.
Ended at last is the labor of love:
Once more through the gateway the saddened lines
   move—
A wailing of anguish, a sobbing of grief,
Falls low on the ear of the battle-scared chief;
Close crouched by the portals, a sunny-haired child
Besought him in accents with grief rendered wild:

"Oh! sir, he was good, and they said he died brave—
Why! why! did you pass by my dear papa's grave?
I know he was poor, but as kind and as true
As ever marched into the battle with you—
His grave is so humble, no stone marks the spot,
You may not have seen it. Oh, say you did not!
For my poor heart will break if you knew he was there,
And thought him too lowly your offerings to share.
He didn't die lowly—he poured his heart's blood,
In rich crimson streams, from the top-crowning sod
Of the breastworks which stood in front of the fight—
And died shouting 'Onward! for God and the right!'

O'er all his dead comrades your bright garlands wave,
But you haven't put *one* on *my* papa's grave.
If mamma were here—but she lies by his side,
Her wearied heart I roke when our dear papa died."

" Battalion ! file left ! countermarch !" cried the chief.
"This young orphan'd maid hath full cause for her
    grief."
Then up in his arms from the hot, dusty street,
He lifted the maiden, while in through the gate
The long line repasses, and many an eye
Pays fresh tribute of tears to the lone orphan's sigh.
" This way it is—here, sir—right under this tree :
They lie close together, with just room for me."
"Halt ! Cover with roses each lowly green mound—
A love pure as this makes these graves hallowed ground."
"Oh ! thank you, kind sir ! I ne'er can repay
The kindness you've shown little Daisy to-day :
But I'll pray for you here, each day while I live.
'Tis all that a poor soldier's orphan can give.

I shall see papa soon, and dear mamma too—
I dreamed so last night, and I know 'twill come true ;
And they will both bless you, I know, when I say
How you folded your arms round their dear one to-day—
How you cheered her sad heart, and soothed it to rest,
And hushed its wild throbs on your strong noble breast ;
And when the kind angels shall call *you* to come,
We'll welcome you there to our beautiful home,
Where death never comes, his black banners to wave,
And the beautiful flowers ne'er weep o'er a grave."
                —*C. E. L. Holmes.*

THE RAVEN.

ONCE upon a midnight dreary, while I pondered,
    weak and weary,
Over many a quaint and curious volume of forgotten
    lore,—
While I nodded, nearly napping, suddenly there came a
    tapping,
As of some one gently rapping, rapping at my chamber
    door.
"'Tis some visitor," I mutter'd, "tapping at my chamber
    door—
       Only this, and nothing more."

Ah distinctly I remember, it was in the bleak December,
And each separate dying ember wrought its ghost upon
the floor.
Eagerly I wished the morrow ; vainly I had sought to
borrow
From my books surcease of sorrow—sorrow for the lost
Lenore,—
For the rare and radiant maiden whom the angels name
Lenore—
Nameless here forevermore.

And the silken, sad. uncertain rustling of each purple
curtain,
Thrilled me,—filled me with fantastic terrors never felt
before ;
So that now, to still the beating of my heart, I stood re-
peating,
" 'Tis some visitor entreating entrance, at my chamber-
door,—
Some late visitor entreating entrance at my chamber-
door :
That is is, and nothing more."

Presently my soul grew stronger; hesitating then no
longer,
"Sir," said I, "or Madam, truly your forgiveness I implore ;
But the fact is, I was napping, and so gently you came
rapping,
And so faintly you came tapping, tapping at my cham-
ber-door,
That I scarce was sure I heard you"—here I opened wide
the door :
Darkness there, and nothing more.

Deep into that darkness peering, long I stood there, won-
dering, fearing.
Doubting. dreaming dreams no mortals ever dared to
dream before ;
But the silence was unbroken, and the stillness gave no
token,
And the only word there spoken was the whispered
word, "Lenore !"
This I whispered, and an echo murmured back the word,
"LENORE !"
Merely this and nothing more.

Back into the chamber turning, all my soul within me
burning,
Soon again I heard a tapping, something louder than before.
"Surely," said I, "surely that is something at my win-
dow-lattice ;
Let me see then what thereat is and this mystery ex-
plore,—
Let my heart be still a moment, and this mystery ex-
plore—
 'Tis the wind, and nothing more."

Open here I flung the shutter, when, with many a flirt
and flutter,
In there stepped a stately raven of the saintly days of
yore.
Not the least obeisance made he ; not a minute stopped
or stayed he :
But, with mien of lord or lady, perched above my cham-
ber-door,—
Perched upon a bust of Pallas, just above my chamber-
door—
 Perched and sat, and nothing more.

Then this ebony bird beguiling my sad fancy into smiling,
By the grave and stern decorum of the countenance it
wore,
"Though thy crest be shorn and shaven, thou," I said,
"art sure no craven :
Ghastly, grim, and ancient raven, wandering from the
nightly shore,
Tell me what thy lordly name is on the night's Plutonian
shore?"
 Quoth the raven, "Nevermore !"

Much I marveled this ungainly fowl to hear discourse
so plainly,
Though its answer little meaning, little relevancy bore ;
For we cannot help agreeing that no living human being
Ever yet was blessed with seeing bird above his cham-
ber-door,
Bird or beast upon the sculptured bust above his cham-
ber-door
 With such name as "Nevermore !"

But the raven, sitting lonely on the placid bust, spoke
only

That one word, as if his soul in that one word he did
   outpour.
Nothing further then he uttered ; not a feather then he
   fluttered—
Till I scarcely more than muttered, "Other friends have
   flown before,
On the morrow he will leave me, as my hopes have flown
   before,
      Then the bird said, " Nevermore !"

Startled at the stillness, broken by reply so aptly spoken,
" Doubtless," said I, "what it utters is its only stock and
   store,
Caught from some unhappy master, whom unmerciful
   disaster
Follow'd fast and follow'd faster, till his songs one bur-
   den bore,
Till the dirges of his hope that melancholy burden bore,"
      Of—' Never—nevermore !"

But the raven still beguiling all my sad soul into smiling,
Straight I wheeled a cushioned seat in front of bird and
   bust and door,
Then, upon the velvet sinking, I betook myself to linking
Fancy unto fancy, thinking what this ominous bird of
      yore—
What this grim, ungainly, ghastly, gaunt, and ominous
   bird of yore
      Meant in croaking " Nevermore !"

Thus I sat engaged in guessing, but no syllable expressing
To the fowl whose fiery eyes now burned into my bosom's
   core :
This and more I sat divining, with my head at ease re-
   clining
On the cushion's velvet lining that the lamplight gloated
   o'er,
But whose velvet violet lining with the lamplight gloat-
   ing o'er
      She shall press—ah ! nevermore !

Then methought the air grew denser, perfumed from an
   unseen censer,
Swung by seraphim, whose foot-falls tinkled on the
   tufted floor,
"Wretch," I cried, "thy God hath lent thee—by these
   angels he hath sent thee

Respite—respite and nepenthe from thy memories of
Lenore !
Quaff, oh quaff this kind nepenthe, and forget this lost
Lenore !"
    Quoth the raven "Nevermore !"

" Prophet !" said I, "thing of evil !—prophet still, if
bird or devil !
Whether tempter sent, or whether tempest tossed thee
here ashore,
Desolate, yet all undaunted, on this desert land en-
chanted—
On this home by horror haunted—tell me truly, I implore,—
Is there –is there balm in Gilead ?—tell me—tell me, I
implore !"
    Quoth the raven, "Nevermore !"

"Prophet !" said I, " thing of evil !—prophet still, if bird
or devil !
By that heaven that bends above us, by that God we
both adore,
Tell this soul, with sorrow laden, if within the distant
Aidenn,
It shall clasp a sainted maiden, whom the angels name
Lenore ;
Clasp a rare and radient maiden, whom the angels name
Lenore !"
    Quoth the raven, " Nevermore !"

" Be that word our sign of parting, bird or fiend !" I
shrieked, upstarting,—
"Get thee back into the tempest and the night's Plutonian shore.
Leave no black plume as a token of that lie thy soul hath
spoken !
Leave my loneliness unbroken !—quit the bust above my
door !
Take thy beak from out my heart, and take thy form
from off my door !"
    Quoth the raven, " Nevermore !"

And the raven, never flitting, still is sitting, still is sitting
On the pallid bust of Pallas, just above my chamber-
door :

And his eyes have all the seeming of a demon's that is
    dreaming,
And the lamp-light o'er him streaming throws his
    shadow on the floor ;
And my soul from out that shadow that lies floating on
    the floor
Shall be lifted—nevermore !

                    —Edgar A. Poe.

THE KNIGHT OF ST. CRISPIN,

OR THE LEARNED COBBLER.

I'VE read somewhere, how once in by-gone days
    That common cobblers took to learned ways,
Well posted up in things of church and state ;
How glib they were in scientific prate,
Each in his turn, for others spoke and read,
Who pegged away and noted what was said,
But now I have a modern cobbler in my mind
That leaves all *ancient* cobblers far behind.
A finer Crispin never made a fit
A better cobbler sure, a sprig ne'er hit,
A bigger slouch ne'er lived since time began,
And yet, beneath those rags there breathed a *man.*
No theologic point for him too fine,
Nor deep, not e'en the Trinity Divine.
His faith was firm in trans-substantiation.
To doubt was sin enough to damn a nation.
Defended loud and well Old Erin's cause,
Disputed England's right to frame her laws.
He worshipped " Ford," and eager read his " World ; "
And then he doubly damned the N. **Y.** Herald.
He rose not early, but he worked full late,
And when his "crowd" came in, he rose in state,
And with the eloquence of great St. Paul,
His words poured forth, he vanquished all.
He had his patrons, some on gilt-edge list,
But some were bad, their very names he hissed.
" There's James Galbraith, he's true in all his ways,
His word's a bond, you may depend on what he says.
When work is done his money's on the mark.
There's Tom Mulvey, what shall I say, the shark.
His boots are done—three months they're on my hand—
Just what to do with him I'm at a stand ;

I wish I had, I swear, his well-tanned skin :
I swear I'd like to draw the waxed-end in.
It's on the 'beat' he is—I wish him luck :
Just wait! some time I'll nab me Laddy Buck."
This cobbler had a vixen of a wife,
That proved a very terror to his life.
She'd give him H—l, and then skip out
And leave two bairns for him to clean and clout.
How oft 'tis thus with men of heart and mind,
In things de-cour, to get sore left behind.
What pearls attend the married state
When Wisdom speaks, but speaks too late.
'Tis not in grace to keep that wedlock straight
Where young Miss Early weds to Mr. Late.
For he who marries much beneath his years,
Takes worlds and worlds of risk on eyes and ears ;
But then John's nuptials booded much of ill,
The bliss John sought, poor John is seeking still.
He had, 'tis true, the lady's full consent,
But when he turned his back. the lady went ;
For from the ordinary course of love
Did John's the least exception prove.
But he got round as quiet as a mouse,
The Squire was summoned to his humble house.
He came with legal mein and earnest look,
He carried too, a pen and ink and book.
He said " we're here, for haste there is no need,
But if all things are ready, we'll proceed."
The groom looked anxious round and then replied,
" The Squire, the witness, all I lack's the bride."
The Squire now turned and went his way,
"Go, catch the bird, I'll come another day
He said, and I'll come straightway down
And e'er the birdie flies I'll make you one.
In this grave fact we all must coincide,
There is no wedding where there is no bride."
The would-be groom, now searched through all the night
And found the truant damsel near daylight.
But now the Squire was soundly napping so
He'd dreamed and dreamed of some one rapping so
That night upon his bed-room window pane,
And thinking 'twas a dream he dozed again :
But morning came—the Squire was prompt on hand,
The witness, bride and groom were on the stand.
They both were pledged for better or for worse,
The sequel proves *she* was a bitter curse.
For what she never knew she would contend,
Till waxing loud, all peace was at an end.
She said one day she hoped to die

If ought she ever met to clean a house
Was half so good as consecrated lie."
John stared at such expression from his spouse,
He suggested concentrate for consecrate,
But she maintained her word appropriate,
From angry words they came to angry blows,
And John was left to nurse a bloody nose.
His church admitting no divorce,
He grabbed the broom and drove her out by force.
Oh! how we grieve when things oppose our mind,
But in the lapse of after years we find
How kindly were the rulings left to fate
Those fancied pleasures that we'd scarce forego
Oft prove a curse and fill our lives with woe.
John's troubles came when he expected least,
Then for relief he sought the parish priest.
The priest, a man quite young in years,
Allayed the cobbler's greatest fears.
It was too much for John upon the whole
Two care two bairns for flesh and soul :
He for his children would asylum find,
With food and care just suited to his mind.
I saw the cobbler late that very night :
By his contented face saw all was right.
He lit his pipe, his sorrows rolled away in smoke;
He crossed his legs, and thus this cobbler spoke :
" Say, Jim, howe'er they may, let skeptics rave,
Religion is a d—d good thing to have.
May'be we'er right to-day, but how's to-morrow ?
But this we know, it comforts us in sorrow.
I've seen in full, life's vanity and shame,
And as for me, 'tis but a *life* in *name*.
When all seems going for the best 'tis loss,
Our gold, though durable, it seems, is dross.
Our sorrows make our hearts more mellow still,
Our care should be to heed our fellow's ill
Through all, a work of justice and of love,
And for the rest we'll trust the Man Above."
—*Anonymous.*

TO A LADY FRIEND.

I HAVE in my window a sweet little rosebud in
bloom,
I think this little rosebud's not blooming alone for me,
So i'll woo it to wait till Minnie, sweet Minnie comes
home,
For somehow or other it seems to be blooming for thee.

SOME TENDER LOINS.

A BUTCHER loved a tender maid,
  To woo her were his designs,
And he sent her copies of tender verse,
  In fact, real tenderloins.

The girl, alas! he could not suet,
  She would love him as a brother,
But when implored to marry, said,
  "Tripe, please, and find another."

The butcher still pursued the girl,
  His pleas became much bolder:
The girl at last, to find relief,
  Gave him a cold shoulder.

He knew then that his hopes were vain,
  But as he left her said,
"Since you have caused me such distress,
  I'll haunch you when I'm dead."

He tried in drink to drown his cares,
  And there found no relief,
But daily grew more woe begone,
  You never sausage grief.

At last his weary soul found rest,
  His sorrows now are o'er:
No fickle maid now troubles him,
  Pork reacher, he's no more.

MY LITTLE WIFE.

SHE isn't very pretty
  (So say my lady friends):
    She's neither wise nor witty
      With verbal odds and ends.

  No fleeting freaks of Fashion
    Accross her fancy run,
  She's never in a passion—
    Except a tender one.

Her voice is low and cooing:
  She listens more than speaks;
While others talk of doing,
  The duty near she seeks.

It may be but to burnish
  The sideboard's scanty plate,
Or but with bread to furnish
  The beggar at the gate.

So I who see what graces
  She sheds on lowly life,
To Fashion's fairest faces
  Prefer my little wife.

And though at her with pity
  The city dames may smile,
Who deem her hardly pretty
  And sadly out of style—

To me she seems a creature
  So musically sweet,
I would not change one feature—
  One curve from crown to feet.

And if I could be never
  Her lover and her mate,
I think I'd be forever
  The beggar at the gate.

          —*H. W. Austin.*

TAKING TOLL.

IN the door of the mill stood Richard Lee,
  White as an image of snow was he,
From his heavy boots to his beautiful lips,
From the crown of his hat to his finger-tips.

Now, slowly jogging along the street,
Drove farmer Brown with his grist of wheat,
And with him Bessie, fresh as the spring,
And ripe as the fruits the fall months bring.

While the farmer drove about the town,
Young Lee ground the wheat and bolted it down;
With many a glance at the maiden fair,
Who sat by the door in the oaken chair.

At last he called her in shouting tones,
And she stood by the whirling, rumbling stones,
And watched the grain as it ebbed so still,
Till the farmer came, but the noise of the mill

Drowned the sound of his feet, and over the hopper
Two heads were bent, and when Richard Lee
Saw him standing there he stammered, " I—see—

That is"—then he paused and shuffled his feet,
" I think there are weevils in your wheat!"
But the farmer smiled and said, " Well, Bess,
Of the two evils always choose the less."

And the maiden looked down confused and meek,
With a patch of flour on one cheek!
Still the old man didn't take it ill,
For he knew young Richard owned the mill.

But he mused as they slowly rode away :
" Well! I've been to the mill now many a day—
Say forty odd years—but bless my soul,
That chap beats all of them taking toll."

THE DYING SHOEMAKER.

DEAR WIFE, I'm waxing near my end,"
    The dying cobbler said :
Soon to an upper world my sole
    Its lonely way must thread.

    " I fear, indeed, I'm pegging out ;
        But then what boots it, love ?
    Here we've been a well-fitted pair,
        And so we'll be above.

    " My ills I know no drugs may heel,
        So its welt to prepare ;
    We can't run counter to our fate—
        Just put a peg in there !

    " The future need not give you care,
        I've left my awl to you ;
    For deep within my inner sole,
        I know that you've been true.

" I've always given you your rights,
    But now you must be left :
However, do not grieve too much
    When of me you're bereft.

" A-last farewell I now will take,"
    He smiled and raised his head :
" B-last the cruel malady
    That lays you low," she said.

" I'll slipper way in peace." he sighed,
    "The strife will soon be past."
His head fell back, he sweetly smiled,
    And then he breathed his last.

THE OLD TIN DINNER PAIL.

[This poem, now published for the first time, was
written by JAMES HOLDEN, of Oswego, N. Y., in 1858,
who carried his dinner pail to and fro for two years, a
distance of four miles.]

HOW dear to me is my tin pail,
    We've traveled long together,
Through wind and rain and snow and hail,
    And dark and dreary weather.

My pail with earthly bounties stored,
    My daily wants supply,
With best the pantry can afford
    Or factory orders buy.

When by fatigue my strength doth fail,
    I to my pail resort,
    I'm sure to find in my tin pail
Refreshments and support.

Sweet pies and cakes of choicest kind,
    Within its bosom hid,
And best of bread I always find,
    When I take off the lid.

Perchance an apple stowed away,
    Or cookies sweet and round,
Or tarts or sweetmeats every day,
    In my tin pail are found.

And now and then a chicken's leg,
   Or choice piece of the breast,
And every day a fresh-laid egg,
   Just taken from the nest.

One favor of some friend I crave,
   When life on earth shall fail.
'Mongst friendship's other tokens, save
   My old tin dinner pail.

Then may it hang both night and day,
   Upon some hook or nail,
And let it not with rust decay,
   But spare that old tin pail.

THE BACHELOR'S NEW YEAR SOLILOQUY.

I STAND to-night like one upon some elevated plain,
   And from that height in thought review life's
     traveled road again.
I'm forty years and three to-night ! how time does steal
     away !
And yet the dreams of youth seem like some dream of
     yesterday.

Here from this height I view some years like hills aglow
     with light ;
These represent those happy years to me of swift-
     winged flight.
And then I see some years like hills, low hung with dark-
     est cloud ;
Those years of sorrow, years that sorrow, covered as a
     shroud.

The brightest views I get, a shadow here and there ap-
     pears,
Just as in youth our brightest hours were dimmed by
     childhood's tears.
I have no doubt that there are years well known to most
     all men,
That they would not recall or wish to live them o'er
     again.

But here I am, this dying hour of eighteen eighty-one,
Soon numbered with forgotten years, those years long
     fled and gone.

Yes, here I am, not sad, though lone I am, in truth to-
night,
My room is neat and clean, and all around me cheery
bright.

My clock there ticks a drowsy tick upon the mantel
shelf,
Reminding me that life with me is passing away itself.
No kindred spirit near me now, but single. free, alone,
No echo to my voice except that echo, all one's own.

My thoughts run smooth as polished slides through finely polished grooves,
Not worried the least by hate, nor maddened by jealous
loves.
But why am I alone to-night, so lonely here to-night,
And why my hopes, those hopes once fond, all doomed
to cruel blight ?

The dearest thing in all this world I think, is a child to me,
Yet likely I'll never know the bliss of children at my
knee.
With mingling of sadness I watch them and share in
their play ;
'Tis like a gleam of fair Spring-time on a chill Winter's
day.

I sometimes feel sad to be lone, but I'm glad to be free,
For pleasure's an offset, the balance now favoring me.
I go where I please, and return when I'm ready, the
same,
And no jealous housewife to curse me and blaspheme
my name.

Forbid that I ever should see my child in want of bread,
Or ever the pride of my heart lie cold and pale and dead.
But woman, dear woman, that riddle, that puzzle to me,
When hearts are at stake and wit's in the scale I'll bet on
a *she*.

Yet one thing I've noticed while jogging along through
life,
The bigger the Devil the man, the more the angel, his
wife
For everything seeks for a balance, a rule since time be
gan,
How often we find a termagant tied to the kindest man.

But why will a woman take and stick, stick for a vil-
lain's part,
When an honest man might sue in vain, in vain for her
heart.
Her heart goes out to the rake in the criminal box;
She'll pity and throw herself away on a Chastine Cox.

I've looked it all carefully over the best that I can,
The conclusion is this, that woman's the savior of man.
When adversity frowns, and passed by his fellows un-
blessed,
He turns him in despond to woman and often finds rest.

I promised in life's early day, when my race in life began,
That never would I mislead a woman, " God's best gift
to man."
And glad I'm that in all candor and conscience I can
say,
That I have kept my promise right up to the present day.

To all good-night, good-night, for here my reveries must
close,
For Nature calls for a kind, a kind and a sweet repose.
The bells have been ringing a sad farewell to the year
just gone,
A sad farewell to the dying year, to the year eighty-one.
They'll ring again with a changeful tune, all cheerful
and new,
They'll ring out a welcome, a welcome to the year
eighty-two.

—Anonymous.

SELF-CONVICTED.

YOU horrid fellow ! how ever did you dare
    To kiss me in that fashion, disarrange my hair ?
You take undue advantage, no one being present,
And kiss me—oh, how rude ! (but awful pleasant).

" I told you once before it wasn't nice,
And yet, not satisfied with that, you kissed me twice.
Now don't do so again, for ma will hear you,
And she'll come in and find me near you.

"Why don't I move away? Quite easy that to answer;
I'm not so timid—though a female—understand, sir!
You would not think me brave if I retreated,
So here 1 shall remain, though but to be defeated.

"My face is flushed I know—*the air is stifling!*
But why do you persist in this vain, silly trifling?
You must not kiss again! I beg—implore!
And ma may hear—*so I will close the door.*

DEPARTED HOPES.

The following original lines were written by a young
lady a short time before her death. The original copy
was sent to her mother in this city.

MY hopes have departed forever,
    My vision of *true* love is o'er;
My heart can awaken—oh! never;
    There's joy for my bosom no more.
The roses that crowned me are blighted.
    The garlands I cherished are dead,
And the faith once confidingly plighted
    Is broken—my loved one has fled!

They saw that my life was decaying,
    They knew that my stay would be brief,
And still though my spirit was straying
    I told not a word of my grief;
No whisper revealed my deceiver.
    No ear heard me sigh or complain;
Yet my heart still adored its undoer
    And I longed so to meet him again.

He came, but another had rifled
    His heart of the love once my own;
I grieved, but my anguish was stifled,
    After all my soul's idol *is stone!*
The sun is now sinking in billows
    Of clouds in the bleak wintry west,
And morning will shine thro' the willows,
    And find me forever at rest.

This is regarded as one of the most remarkable cases
of the kind on record, and teaches a moral lesson no
young lady can afford to disregard.

GROWN APART

ONE in name, yet two in heart,
　Slowly, but surely, grown apart :
Saddest of all sad sights to see—
Love from his own sweet bonds set free.

Grown apart through the lagging years—
Nor smiles, nor sighs, nor melting tears,
Shall call love's rose to the cheek again,
Or thrill the heart with its precious pain.

Growing apart—for evermore—
A canker-worm at the very core,
Shorn of all the sweets of life :
An unloved husband, unloved wife.

Ah well ! they have had their little day :
Some flowers bloom only, and die in May :
And if these have missed the Summer's prime,
And riper fruits of the Autumn time ;

Knowing only the drought of one,
And failing the other's blasts to shun :
There yet may be garnered in each sad heart,
Sheaves that have ripened and grown apart.
　　　　　　　　—*Charlotte Lennox.*

BLESSED DREAMS.

THE sunset smile has left the sky,
　The moon rose calm and fair,
As low a little maiden knelt
　To breathe her nightly prayer,
And thus her brief petition rose,
　In simple words and few ;
"Dear Lord, please send us blessed dreams,
　And let them all come true."

Oh ! I have stood in temples grand,
　Where in the rainbow gloom
Rose pompous prayers from priestly lips
　Through clouds of sweet perfume.
But never one has seemed to me
　So guileless, pure and new—

" Dear Lord, please send us blessed dreams,
  And let them all come true."

Ah ! little maiden, kneeling there
  Beneath the sunset skies,
What need have we of other prayer
  Than yours, so sweet and wise !
Henceforth I breathe no studied plea,
  But bow and humbly pray with you—
" Dear Lord, please send us pleasant dreams,
  And let them all come true."

INDEX.

	Page
Acrostic	26
An Idyl	22–23
Blessed Are They That Mourn	42–43
Blessed Dreams	61–62
Brief Sayings	27–34
Departed Hopes	60
Elegiac Poem	9–10
Farewell to the Tuna	20
Fallen	37–40
Grown Apart	61
Hope	16–17
I'll Ne'er Forget My Nannie, O	23–24
I'll No Regret My Nannie, O	8
In Perplexity	4–7
My Little Wife	53–54
Newsboy's Greeting, No. 1	17
Newsboy's Greeting, No. 2	18
New Year's Eve	42
Rather Pointed	24–25
Satire on Woman	10–13
Self-Convicted	59–60
Sing That Song For Me Again	25–26
Smiling Through Our Tears	18–19
Some Things Sad to See	13
Some Tender Loines	53
Taking Toll	54–55
Thanatopsis	40–41
The Bachelor's New Year's Soliloquy	57–59
The Bonnie Belles O' Bradford, No 1	14
The Bonnie Belles of Bradford, No. 2	19
The Bonnie Hills of Bradford	14–15
The Dying Shoemaker	55–56
The Evolution of Temperance	20–21
The Knight of St. Cryspan	50–52
The Old Tin Dinner Pail	56–57
The Orphan's Plea	21–22
The Pebble in the Ocean	15
The Pilot Ship	7–8
The Raven	45–50
The River Time	43–44
To a Lady Friend	52
Who Sent Thee to Bloom	16
You Put No Flowers on Papa's Grave	44–45

www.ingramcontent.com/pod-product-compliance
Lightning Source LLC
Chambersburg PA
CBHW032046090426
42733CB00030B/712